WHAT IF YOU HAD
ANIMaL FEET!?

by Sandra Markle

Illustrated by
Howard McWilliam

Scholastic Inc.

For
Luke Ronald Zabel
and his special
grandparents
Ron and
Pat Zabel

Text copyright © 2015 by Sandra Markle
Illustrations copyright © 2015 by Howard McWilliam

All rights reserved. Published by Scholastic Inc. SCHOLASTIC and associated logos are trademarks and/or registered trademarks of Scholastic Inc.

ISBN 978-0-545-73312-0

12 11 10 9 8 7 6 5 4 3   15 16 17 18 19 20/0

Printed in the U.S.A.   40
First printing, January 2015
Art direction by Paul W. Banks
Design by Kay Petronio

What if one day when you woke up and climbed out of bed, the feet you planted on the floor weren't yours? What if, overnight, a wild animal's feet took their place at the end of your legs?

EASTERN GRAY
KANGAROO

An eastern gray kangaroo's hind feet are super big—just the sole of an adult's foot can be 18 inches long. Big feet help a kangaroo jump about 30 feet in a single hop. Each huge jump means a kangaroo can cover a lot of ground *fast*.

FACT

Eastern gray kangaroos live in groups called mobs. When one kangaroo senses danger, it thumps its hind feet on the ground to warn the others.

If you had eastern gray kangaroo hind feet, you'd be able to jump up as high as six feet, so you could reach high shelves with ease.

HOUSEFLY

A housefly's feet have tiny claws for gripping. Plus, they have footpads covered with hairlike parts that give off a gluey substance. So a fly sticks where it lands—even upside down on the ceiling!

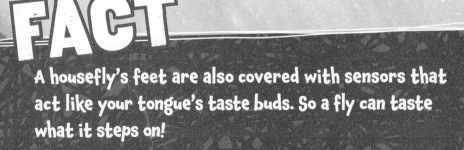

FACT

A housefly's feet are also covered with sensors that act like your tongue's taste buds. So a fly can taste what it steps on!

If you had housefly feet, you'd be a basketball superstar. You could run up the wall and across the ceiling to drop the ball through the hoop. You'd never miss a shot!

GREEN BASILISK LIZARD

A green basilisk lizard's back feet have long toes fringed with skin. This fringe spreads out when it slaps its foot down. When it slaps its foot on water, air becomes trapped under each toe. And when it runs fast, this keeps the lizard on the surface for at least 15 feet.

FACT

When it sinks underwater, a green basilisk lizard's fringed toes become great swim fins.

If you had green basilisk lizard feet, you wouldn't need a bridge to cross a stream, and you'd be on the other side in no time!

CHEETAH

A cheetah's foot is made up of soft pads—a center one and toe pads—plus nails. Shaped like that, it has a new name: instead of a foot, it's called a paw. A cheetah's paw pads are tough and ridged like tire treads and the cheetah's sturdy nails act like cleats. So its paws keep it from slipping during superfast sprints. These amazing paws help a cheetah run as fast as 70 miles per hour. That's faster than any other land animal!

FACT

A cheetah's pattern of footpad ridges are as unique as a fingerprint, which means no two cheetahs have the same paws.

If you had cheetah feet, you'd be on time for school every day because you'd always catch the bus!

GRAY WOLF

A gray wolf's feet are called paws, too. When crossing snow, a gray wolf's toes separate and stretch apart. That makes its paws bigger and, like wearing snowshoes, spreads out its weight. This means its paws don't sink in as deep, which makes walking or running easier.

FACT

A special network of tiny blood vessels helps keep a wolf's feet warm even on ice.

If you had gray wolf feet, you could play barefoot in the snow and still have toasty-warm tootsies.

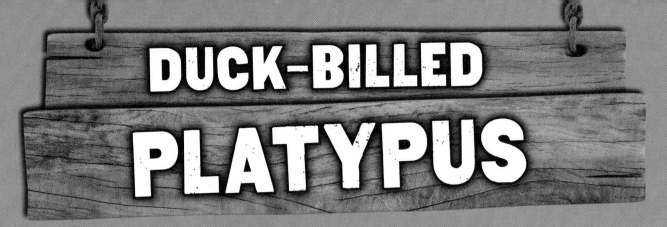

DUCK-BILLED PLATYPUS

A duck-billed platypus has skin connecting its spread-apart toes. This type of foot is called a webbed foot. The platypus's front feet even have skin that sticks out beyond its toes, making them the perfect swimming flippers. But the minute it starts to walk, dig, or scratch, this skin pulls back so the platypus can use its sturdy, sharp nails.

FACT

A male duck-billed platypus's back feet each have a spur-like nail to inject venom, a poisonous fluid. This isn't deadly to humans but can be very painful.

If you had duck-billed platypus feet, you'd be a fast-swimming superhero with a built-in weapon.

BARN OWL

A barn owl's feet have four toes tipped with talons, which are long, curved, sharp nails. Usually, three of its toes aim forward and one backward. But it can swing a second toe on each foot to the back. This helps keep an extra-tight grip on wiggly prey, such as rats or mice.

FACT

A barn owl's middle front toenail on each foot has a toothlike edge. It uses this to comb the feathers on its disk-shaped face. Flat feathers funnel sound into its ears so it can listen as well as watch when hunting for a meal.

If you had barn owl feet, you'd never have to bend over to pick things up.

AARDVARK

Each of the toes on an aardvark's feet ends in a sharp, sturdy toenail—the front ones are shovel-shaped. These are great for digging a burrow for their home or finding ants and termites, its favorite foods.

FACT

If attacked by a predator, like a lion or leopard, an aardvark digs a burrow to escape. If caught, it flips onto its back and lashes out with its nails.

If you had aardvark feet, you could dig super fast, which means you'd be the first to find buried treasure.

GIANT AFRICAN MILLIPEDE

A giant African millipede's body is made up of segments. A baby starts out with just four or five segments, but as it grows it adds on more. Each segment has about four feet. An adult may be forty segments long, with lots of feet, and it needs every single one. It can travel by tunneling through the ground. So while some feet are busy walking, others move dirt out of its way.

FACT

A giant African millipede has an exoskeleton, meaning the hard parts of its body are on the outside. So to defend itself, it curls up with its delicate legs and feet inside and its armor outside.

With giant African millipede feet, you wouldn't need anyone else to have a parade. You would be a marching band of one!

MOUNTAIN GOAT

A mountain goat's foot is encased in a hard nail-like covering. Shaped that way, it has a special name: instead of a foot, it's called a hoof. A mountain goat's hoof is split in two halves. And each can move separately. That lets it get a good grip in rocky, high places.

FACT

Each half of a mountain goat's hoof has a sharp edge plus a rubbery pad. Together, these add extra grip to keep it from slipping.

If you had mountain goat feet, your feet would be all you need to rescue a kitten.

WHITE RHINOCEROS

Each white rhinoceros foot is an elastic pad plus three stiff toes tipped with hoof-like nails. With each step, its footpad presses down, spreading the toes wide apart. This lets the rhino's feet support its heavy body. And it needs the support! Adult rhinos can weigh as much as 7,000 pounds.

FACT

In spite of their size, white rhinos can run as fast as 30 miles per hour. But only over short distances.

If you had
white rhinoceros
feet, your family wouldn't
need a car because you
could carry everyone
all at once.

Wild animal feet could be cool for a while. But you don't need your feet to grab food, run on water, or stand upside down on the ceiling. And you don't

need your feet to stay well-groomed or taste what you step on. But if you could have wild animal feet for more than a day, which kind would be right for you?

Luckily, you don't have to choose. The feet at the end of your legs will always be people feet. They're what you need to run, walk, dance, skip,

hop, and even just stand in one place. With the right footwear, you can do lots more. Plus, your feet can look very stylish while you're being active.

WHAT'S SPECIAL ABOUT YOUR FEET?

Each of your feet is unique. It's rare for anyone to have two feet that are exactly alike. Toe prints are as unique as fingerprints. And one foot is usually slightly bigger than the other. The *Guinness Book of Records* lists Brahim Takioullah as having the world's biggest feet. His left is 15 inches long; his right is 14.76 inches. No wonder Brahim has to have his shoes specially made for him!

Most important, your feet are built for action. Each foot is made up of twenty-six bones and thirty-three joints, places where bones meet so the body can bend easily. Plus, there are lots of muscles to pull on all of those bones and move them.

KEEP YOUR FEET HEALTHY

Your feet need to be in good condition to do their best for you. So here are some tips for taking care of your feet.

- Choose shoes that fit properly. Ones that are too tight can be painful and cause problems, such as ingrown toenails.

- Be active to exercise your foot muscles and keep your feet flexible. If possible, walk and play on grass or dirt. That's easier on your feet than being on a hard, paved surface.

- Wash and dry your feet daily, especially between your toes. That's the best way to prevent problems like athlete's foot, a fungal infection of the skin. Also check regularly for any cuts, blisters, or open sores. If you see any, ask an adult to help you treat them. If your feet don't heal quickly, you may need to visit a doctor for more care.

- Whenever possible, wear socks with your shoes. Socks help absorb shocks and keep your shoes from rubbing your feet. Feet also sweat a lot and socks soak up sweat. Then, before bacteria have time to attack your feet, change your socks and wash the dirty ones.

PHOTO CREDITS

Photos ©: Animals Animals: 16 main (Ardea/Watson, M.), 22 main (Kettlewell, Richard); Dreamstime: 12 inset (Bambi L. Dingman), cover bottom (Isselee), 18 inset (Lukas Blazek), 20 main (Matthew Bowden); Getty Images: 4 main (Danita Delimont), cover background (Dave Hughes), 4 inset, 8 inset (Ingo Arndt/Foto Natura), 18 main, 32 bottom right (wendy salisbury photography); iStockphoto: 6 main (arlindo71), 10 inset (BirdImages), 24 inset, 32 bottom left (konmesa), 24 main (roberto222); Landov/Mike Segar/Reuters: 16 inset; Minden Pictures: 22 inset, 32 top (Chris & Tilde Stuart), 20 inset (Konrad Wothe); Science Source/Cheryl Power: 6 inset; Shutterstock, Inc.: back cover (Angela Waye), cover top and throughout (Dim Dimich), 12 main (Michelle Lalancette); Superstock, Inc.: 10 main, 14 inset (Minden Pictures), 8 main (NaturePL), 14 main (NHPA).